COPYCAT

RECIPES

Famous Collection of the 50 Most Popular Poultry and Fish Recipes, Created with a Step-by-Step Process by the Best Chefs of the Last Decade.

Carolyn Mitchum

with the express written consent from the Publisher. All additional right reserved.

The information in the following pages is broadly considered a truthful and accurate account of facts and as such, any inattention, use, or misuse of the information in question by the reader will render any resulting actions solely under their purview. There are no scenarios in which the publisher or the original author of this work can be in any fashion deemed liable for any hardship or damages that may befall them after undertaking information described herein. Additionally, the information in the following pages is intended only for informational purposes and should thus be thought of as universal. As befitting its nature, it is presented without assurance regarding its prolonged validity or interim quality. Trademarks that are mentioned are done without written consent and can in no way be considered an endorsement from the trademark holder.

Table of Contents

1. Fish Mappas

Preparation Time: 15 mins

Cooking Time: 20 mins

Easy

Servings: 4

Ingredients:

- 300g basmati rice
- 1 tbsp sunflower or vegetable oil
- 2 large onions , sliced
- 2 garlic cloves , chopped
- 450g tomatoes , cut into chunks
- 3 tbsp tikka curry paste
- 400g can coconut milk
- 4 skinless, boneless pollock fillets (about 150g/ 51/2oz each), or other sustainable white fish, cut into 4cm/11/2in chunks
- ½ small pack coriander , roughly chopped

Directions:

Put a large saucepan of water on to boil and cook the rice following pack instructions. Meanwhile, heat the oil in a large, wide saucepan over a medium heat and add the onions. Cook for 5-10 mins until softened and starting to colour. Add the garlic and tomatoes, and fry for 2 mins. Add the curry paste, fry for 2 mins more, then pour in the coconut milk and bring to the boil.

Add the fish to the pan and simmer gently for 5-8 mins until just cooked through. Turn off the heat. Sprinkle the coriander over the curry and serve with the rice.

Nutrition: per serving

Kcal 691, Fat:26g, Saturates:16g, Carbs:74g, Sugars:11g, Fibre:4g, Protein:39g, Salt:0.8g

2. Easy-to-Scale Cheesy Fish Pie With Kale

Preparation Time: 10 mins

Cooking Time: 45 mins

Easy

Servings: 2

Ingredients:

- 200g Maris Piper potatoes , cut into chunks
- 1 tbsp butter
- 1 tbsp flour
- 200ml whole milk , plus 1 tbsp
- ½ tsp Dijon mustard
- 100g cheddar, gruyère or emmental, grated
- 200g fish pie mix (we used a mix of salmon, haddock and prawns)
- 50g frozen peas
- 50g shredded kale
- 1 spring onion , finely sliced
- 1 tbsp parmesan , finely grated
- green salad , to serve (optional)

Directions:

Tip the potatoes into a pan, cover with hot water from the kettle and add a pinch of salt. Simmer for 15-20 mins until tender, then drain and leave to steam-dry.Meanwhile, warm the butter in a heavy-based pan over a low heat. Add the flour and stir until you have a paste. Gradually whisk in 200ml milk until you have a thick white sauce. Simmer for 3-4 mins, stirring. Season, then stir in the mustard and half the cheese, and continue to stir until the cheese has melted. Fold in the fish, peas and kale, and cook for 8 mins more, or until the kale wilts, the fish is just cooked and the prawns are starting to turn pink. Heat the grill to medium-high. Mash the potatoes with the spring onion and 1 tbsp milk. Fold in the remaining cheese and season well.

Tip the filling into a heatproof dish and spoon the cheesy mash on top, swirling it with a fork until the filling is completely covered. Sprinkle over the parmesan and grill for 10-15 mins until the pie is golden and bubbling. Serve with a green salad, if you like. *Uncooked pie, well covered in the dish, will keep in the freezer for up to three months.*

Nutrition: Per serving

Kcal 634,   Fat: 37g,   Saturates:20g,   Carbs:31g,

Sugars:8g,   Fibre:4g,   Protein:42g,   Salt:1.7g

3.   Spicy Fish Stew

⏳ **Preparation Time:** 10 mins

🕐 **Cooking Time:** 40 mins

👨‍🍳 **Easy**

🍽 **Servings:** 4

Ingredients:

- 1 tbsp olive oil
- 2 onions , thinly sliced
- 3 spring onions , chopped
- 3 garlic cloves , chopped
- 1 red chilli , seeded and thinly sliced
- few thyme sprigs
- 2 x 400g cans chopped tomatoes
- 400ml vegetable bouillon made with 2 tsp vegetable bouillon powder
- 2 green peppers, seeded and cut into pieces
- 160g brown basmati rice

- 400g can and 210g can red kidney beans, drained
- handful fresh coriander, chopped, plus a few sprigs extra
- handful flat-leaf parsley, chopped
- 550g pack frozen wild salmon , skinned and cut into large pieces
- 1 lime , zested

Directions:

Heat the oil in a large non-stick pan and fry the onions for 8-10 mins until softened and golden. Add the spring onions, garlic, chilli and thyme. Cook, stirring, for 1 min. Pour in the tomatoes and bouillon, then stir in the peppers. Cover and leave to simmer for 15 mins. Meanwhile, cook the rice according to pack instructions. Stir in the beans with the coriander and parsley, then leave to cook gently for another 10 mins until the peppers are tender. Add the salmon and lime zest and cook for 4-5 mins until cooked through.

Ladle half of the stew into two bowls and scatter with the coriander sprigs. Cool the remaining stew, then cover and chill to eat on another night. Gently reheat in a saucepan until bubbling.

Nutrition: per serving

Kcal 664, Fat:26g, Saturates:5g, Carbs:58g, sugars: 14g, high in fibre:14g, high in protein:42g, Salt:0.3g

4. Creamy Leek, Potato, Cheddar & Chive Fish Pie

Preparation Time: 5 mins

Cooking Time: 1 hr plus 30 mins chilling and 15 mins cooling

More effort

Servings: 5 – 6

Ingredients:

- 400g plain flour, plus extra for dusting
- 1 tsp fine salt
- ½ small bunch of thyme, leaves picked
- ½ tbsp English mustard powder
- 180g cold unsalted butter, cut into cubes
- 2 large eggs, beaten
- steamed greens, to serve

For the filling:

- 1 potato (about 270g), chopped into 3cm chunks
- 1 tbsp olive oil
- 50g butter

- 2 leeks, finely sliced
- 3 tbsp plain flour
- 400ml whole milk
- 100ml double cream
- 100g mature cheddar, grated
- 3 tsp Dijon mustard
- ¼ bunch of chives, finely chopped
- 200g skinless salmon fillet, cut into chunks
- 200g skinless smoked haddock fillet, cut into chunks
- 100g raw king prawns, peeled

Directions:

Tip the flour, salt, thyme and mustard powder into a food processor and pulse briefly. Add the butter and pulse again to a fine breadcrumb texture. Add half the egg and 1 tbsp cold water and pulse until it comes together into a dough (you can add up to 1-2 tbsp more water if it's dry). Tip the dough onto a work surface and knead briefly. Wrap and chill for 30 mins. To make the filling, cook the potato in a pan of boiling water for 8-10 mins. Drain and leave to steam-dry. Heat the oil and butter in a large frying pan over a medium heat, and fry the leeks for 5 mins. Stir in the flour and cook for 2 mins, then add the milk, a little at a time, stirring between each addition to combine. Add the cream, cheese and mustard, and cook for 1-2 mins more until the cheese has melted. Stir in the chives and season. Remove from the heat and leave to cool for 15 mins.

Heat the oven to 220C/200C fan/ gas 8. Gently fold the salmon, potato, haddock and prawns into the creamy leek mixture, then spoon into a 27cm round pie dish. Roll the pastry out on a lightly floured surface to the thickness of a £1 coin. Drape the pastry over the pie, then trim the excess. Crimp the edges, then shape the off-cuts to decorate the top, if you like. Brush with the remaining egg, then bake in the centre of the oven for 35-40 mins until golden. Serve with steamed greens.

Nutrition: Per serving (6)
Kcal 964,   Fat:59g,   Saturates:33g,   Carbs:72g,
Sugars:6g,   high in fibre:6g, Protein:34g, Salt:2.2g

5. One-Pot Coconut Fish Curry

⧗ **Preparation Time:** 5 mins

🕐 **Cooking Time:** 25 mins

👨‍🍳 **Easy**

🍽️ **Servings:** 4

Ingredients:

- 1 tbsp sunflower oil, vegetable oil or coconut oil
- 1 onion , chopped
- 1 large garlic clove , crushed
- 1 tsp turmeric
- 1 tsp garam masala
- 1 tsp chilli flakes
- 400ml can coconut milk
- 390g pack fish pie mix
- 200g frozen peas
- 1 lime , cut into wedges
- yogurt and rice, to serve

Directions:

Heat the oil in a large saucepan over a medium heat, add the onion and a big pinch of salt. Gently fry until the onion is translucent, so around 10 mins, then add the garlic and spices. Stir and cook for another minute, adding a splash of water to prevent them sticking. Tip in the coconut milk and stir well, then simmer for 10 mins.

Tip the fish pie mix and the frozen peas into the pan and cook until the peas are bright green and the fish is starting the flake, so around 3 mins. Season and add lime juice to taste. Ladle into bowls and serve with yogurt and rice.

Nutrition: per serving
Kcal 354,   Fat:23g,   Saturates:16g,   Carbs:13g,
Sugars:7g,   Fibre: 5g, Protein:22g,   Salt:0.6g

6. Luxe Fish Pie

Preparation Time: 45 mins

Cooking Time: 1 hr and 10 mins

Easy

Servings: 8

Ingredients:

- 500g thick white fish fillets, such as cod or haddock, unskinned
- 500g thick salmon fillet, unskinned
- 300g smoked haddock (preferably undyed)
- 700ml full fat or semi-skimmed milk
- 1 medium onion, cut into thin wedges
- 2 bay leaves
- 75g butter
- 75g plain flour
- 140g young spinach leaves
- 3 tbsp white wine or vermouth (optional)
- 0.5 small pack dill, roughly chopped

For the cheesy mash topping:

- 1 ½kg potatoes (ideally Maris Piper), cut into even-sized pieces
- 50g butter
- 100g mature cheddar, coarsely grated
- 300ml tub half-fat crème fraîche

Directions:

Place the fish fillets in a large, wide saucepan and pour over the milk. Add the onion wedges and bay leaves, tucking them in around the fish. Bring to a very gentle simmer, then cover with a lid and remove from the heat immediately. Leave to stand and infuse for 10 mins or until the fish is just cooked. Drain the fish in a colander over a large jug to reserve the infused milk, then tip the fish into a bowl. Set aside.

Meanwhile, make the topping. Put the potatoes in a large saucepan of cold water, bring to the boil, then simmer for 15 mins or until the potatoes are soft but not falling apart. Drain well, return to the pan and mash with the butter, half the cheese and the crème fraîche until smooth. Season to taste and set aside.

To finish the filling, melt the butter in a medium saucepan and stir in the flour. Cook for a few secs, then gradually add the infused milk, stirring over a medium heat for 3 mins until the sauce is smooth and thick. Stir in the spinach and wine or vermouth, if using, and cook for 2 mins more. Remove from the heat and stir in the dill. Season to taste.

Heat oven to 200C/180C fan/gas 6. Spoon a third of the sauce into the base of a 3-litre shallow rectangular dish. Scatter half the fish fillets over the sauce, breaking them into chunky pieces and discarding the skin, any stray bones, onion and bay leaves as you go. Pour over another third of the sauce, then top with more fish. Continue the layers once more, finishing with sauce. Spoon the potato over the fish mixture, starting at the edges. Swirl the potato with the back of a spoon and sprinkle over the remaining cheese. Place the dish on a baking tray and bake in the centre of the oven for 45 mins or until the potato is golden and the filling is bubbling.

RECIPE TIP

TO FREEZE:

Assemble the pie, then cover tightly with a double thickness of foil. Seal, label and freeze the uncooked pie for up to 2 months. Thaw in the fridge for 24-48 hrs, depending on the size of your pie, then cook as per the recipe, adding an extra 15-25 mins, until piping hot throughout.

Nutrition: per serving

Kcal 652,   Fat:32g,   Saturates:17g,   Carbs:45g,

Sugars:8g,   Fibre:4g,   Protein:43g,   Salt:1.6g

7.   Fish Pie with Pea & Dill Mash

Preparation Time: 10 mins

Cooking Time: 55 mins

Easy

Servings: 2

Ingredients:

- 375g potatoes , cut into chunks
- 175g leeks , thickly sliced
- 160g frozen peas
- 2 tbsp half-fat crème fraîche
- ½ lemon, zested and juiced
- 2 tbsp chopped fresh dill
- ½ tsp vegetable bouillon powder
- 100g cherry tomatoes, halved
- 250g skinless cod loin, cut into large chunks
- 50g Atlantic prawns (thawed if frozen)
- veg , to serve (optional)

Directions:

Heat oven to 200C/180C fan/gas 6. Cook the potatoes in a pan of boiling water for 10 mins, with the leeks in a covered steamer over the pan.

Remove the steamer, add the peas to the potatoes and cook for 10 mins more. Drain the peas and potatoes, then mash with ½ tbsp crème fraîche, the lemon zest and juice, dill and bouillon.

Arrange the leeks in a shallow ovenproof pie dish (about 18 x 24cm). Add the tomatoes, cod and prawns, then dot over the rest of the crème fraîche. Spoon over the mash, then spread it lightly to the edges with a fork. Bake for 30-35 mins until bubbling round the sides of the dish. Serve with veg, if you like. If you make this ahead and are cooking from cold, bake for about 10 mins longer.

Nutrition: Per serving

low in kcal 412,   low in fat:7g,   saturates:4g,

Carbs:46g,   Sugars:10g,   Fibre:11g,

Protein:37g,   Salt:0.8g

8. Fennel Compote

Preparation Time: 15 mins

Cooking Time: 1 hr and 10 mins

Easy

Servings: 6

Ingredients:

- 100g butter
- 4 large fennel bulbs , thinly sliced
- 1 onion , thinly sliced
- vegetable oil , for frying
- 75g smoked bacon , chopped
- ½ small pack parsley , chopped

Directions:

Heat half the butter in a widebased saucepan until foaming. Add the fennel and onion, and sweat over a low-medium heat for about 1 hr, adding little slices of butter if needed. After 1 hr, increase the heat and keep on cooking down for another 10 mins, stirring occasionally, until caramelised and jammy, and beginning to brown. Put the remaining butter in a separate pan with a splash of vegetable oil and fry the bacon until crisp. Add to the fennel compote along with the parsley, and season to taste. *Will keep for 3 days in an airtight container.*

Nutrition: per serving

Kcal 212, Fat:17g, Saturates:10g, Carbs:6g, Sugars:5g, Fibre:7g, Protein:4g, Salt:0.8g

9. Sautéed Potatoes with Bacon Lardons & Persillade

Preparation Time: 5 mins

Cooking Time: 25 mins

Easy

Servings: 6

Ingredients:

- 1kg potatoes , cut into 2cm/3/4in pieces
- 2 tbsp rapeseed oil
- 300g smoked bacon lardons
- 25g unsalted butter

For the persillade:

- small pack flat-leaf parsley , chopped
- 2 tsp chopped chervil
- 1 tarragon sprig, leaves chopped
- 1 banana shallot , finely chopped
- 2 garlic cloves , crushed

Directions:

In a large saucepan on a high heat, simmer the potatoes for 5 mins in enough water to just cover them, then drain in a colander and leave for 1 min for the steam to escape.

In a small bowl, mix all the ingredients for the persillade together and set aside. Heat the oil in a large frying pan on a high heat, add the lardons and cook for 8-10 mins until lightly caramelised. Add the potatoes, then the butter.

Season with salt and freshly ground black pepper and cook for 10 mins, stirring regularly, until golden brown all over. Spoon out any excess fat and stir in the persillade. Taste and adjust the seasoning if necessary.

Nutrition: per serving

Kcal 321, Fat:17g, Saturates:6g, Carbs:28g, Sugars:1g, Fibre:4g, Protein:13g, Salt:1.4g

10. Ballotine of Pheasant

Preparation Time: 50 mins

Cooking Time: 55 mins

A challenge

Servings: 4 – 6

Ingredients:

- 2 oven-ready pheasants
- 25g soft butter
- 12 rashers smoked streaky bacon

For the stuffing:

- 1 onion , finely chopped
- 2 tsp butter
- 50g prune , soaked in 3 tbsp brandy
- 400g sausagemeat , from 6 whole sausages
- 2 tbsp thyme leaves
- large handful parsley , roughly chopped
- 25g pistachio
- 25g fresh breadcrumb

Directions:

First, make the stuffing. Fry the onion in the butter for 5-10 mins until softened, then leave to cool completely. Thoroughly mix the remaining ingredients in a large bowl, including the cooled onions. If the wings are attached, cut at the first joint (on most butchered birds they will have been removed). Find the wishbone between the neck and the breast, then use a sharp knife to scrape away the flesh around it. Gently pull it out, trying to keep it as one, cut it away and discard.

Place the pheasant, breast side down, on the board. Using a sharp boning knife, see tip, left, cut through the skin to the backbone along the length of the bird. Working down the length of the pheasant, slowly run your knife down against the ribcage, keeping close to the bone and scraping the flesh away from both. Twist out the thigh joints when you get to them.

Very carefully cut away the main carcass. This is where the skin is at its thinnest, so cut carefully as you don't want to nip or pierce the skin.

Open the bird out like a book and lay it, skin-side down, on the board. Season the bird's flesh with salt and pepper then arrange half of the stuffing down the middle of each of the birds in a sausage shape.

Re-form the bird by lifting the sides up and around the stuffing. After you've done one, repeat with the other pheasant. Wrap each pheasant tightly and neatly with bacon so that the bacon goes all the way round the bird and joins on the underside.

Using butcher's string, tie the pheasant at regular intervals around the width. Then tie it once around the length to hold the stuffing in.

Finally, tie the legs together. The pheasant can be prepared to this stage and chilled up to a day ahead.

Heat oven to 200C/ 180C/gas 6. Transfer the pheasant to a roasting tin. Roast for 45-50 mins, basting regularly with the juices from the tin. Finally, cover with foil and rest for about 15 mins. Serve in thick slices with the juices from the pan.

WHAT KNIFE TO USE WHEN BONING PHEASANT

It's best to use a small, sharp boning knife with a blade that curves inwards near the handle. This will give you maximum control when scraping meat away from the bones. Otherwise use a small, sturdy knife.

WHAT STRING TO USE WHEN BONING PHEASANT.

It's important to use robust and heatproof kitchen string (also known as butcher's string) for tying the pheasant, as normal string could burn or melt in the oven, and ruin the dish.

Nutrition: per serving

Kcal 756, b Fat:50g, Saturates:18g, Carbs:16g, Sugars:8g, Fibre:2g, Protein:56g, Salt:3.1g

11. Chicken Lettuce Wraps

Preparation time: 10 Minutes

Cooking Time: 10 Minutes

Servings: 4

Ingredients:

- Lettuce leaves (for the wraps)

- Sugar (1 tsp.) Soy sauce (2 tbsp. + more for serving)
- Rice vinegar (1 tsp.)
- Hoisin sauce (1 tbsp.)
- Cornstarch (2 tsp.)
- Rice noodles (1 oz.)
- Diced water chestnuts (8 oz. can.)
- Diced green onions (4)
- Diced garlic cloves (3)
- Chili paste (2 tsp.)
- Baby Bella mushrooms (o.75 cup diced)
- Vegetable oil - divided (4 tbsp.)
- Ground chicken breast (1 lb.)

Directions:

Heat a wok using the high-temperature setting and two tablespoons of vegetable oil.

Toss in the ground chicken and cook until the pink is gone. Set aside in a covered dish for now. Pour the remainder of oil into the wok and warm using high heat. When it's hot, toss in the water chestnuts, mushrooms, garlic, green onions, and chili paste. Simmer and stir (2 min.). Return the chicken to wok. Whisk the vinegar, soy sauce, cornstarch, hoisin, and sugar. Add the mixture to the wok and cook for one more minute. Remove from the burner and set aside. Warm one inch of oil in a skillet. Break apart and drop the noodles into the hot oil. Cook the noodles for one minute until they're crispy - not browned.

Drain on a paper towel-lined platter.

Nutrition:

Calorie: 730 kcal,   Fat: 27 g,   Carbs: 81 g,
Sodium: 2050 mg,   Protein: 38 g

12. Famous Dave's Cedar Plank Salmon

⧗ **Preparation time:** 15 minutes

🕐 **Cooking time:** 20 minutes

🍽 **Servings**: 4

Ingredients:

- 2 (12") untreated cedar boards
- 3 ¾ tablespoons of vegetable oil
- 1 tablespoon of rice vinegar
- ¾ teaspoon of sesame oil
- 3 ¾ tablespoons of soy sauce
- 2 ⅔ tablespoons green onion, chopped
- 2 teaspoons fresh ginger root, grated
- ¾ teaspoon garlic, chopped
- 1 ¼ (2 lbs.) skinless salmon fillets

Directions:

Soak the cedar boards for at least 1 hour in warm water. Dive more if you have time; In a shallow dish, mix vegetable oil, rice vinegar, sesame oil, soy sauce, green onion, ginger, and garlic; Put the salmon fillets in the marinade and turn to the coating. Carefully cover and marinate for 15 minutes or up to an hour;

Preheat an outdoor grill over medium heat. Set the plates on the grid. The plates are ready when they start smoking and pop a little;

Set the salmon fillets on the boards and discard the marinade-cover and grill for about 20 minutes. The fish is cooked when you can scale it with a fork. It will continue to cook after removing it from the grill.

Nutrition:

Calorie: 220 kcal,   Fat: 10 g,   Carbs: 5 g,
Sodium: 320 mg,   Protein: 28 g

13. Aussie Chicken

⌛ **Preparation Time:** 25 minutes

🕐 **Cooking time**: 1h20m

🍴 **Servings:** 4

Ingredients:

- 4 skinless, boneless chicken breast halves - pounded to 1/2 inch thickness
- 2 tsps. Seasoning salt
- 6 slices bacon, cut in half
- 1/2 cup prepared yellow mustard
- 1/2 cup honey
- 1/4 cup light corn syrup
- 1/4 cup mayonnaise
- 1 tbsp. dried onion flakes
- 1 tbsp. vegetable oil
- 1 cup sliced fresh mushrooms
- 2 cups shredded Colby-Monterey Jack cheese
- 2 tbsps. Chopped fresh parsley

Directions:

Rub seasoning salt all over the chicken breasts. Cover and place in the refrigerator to chill for 30 minutes.

Preheat oven to 175°C/350°F. Place a large, deep skillet over medium high heat, add bacon and cook until crisp, then set bacon aside. Combine dried onion flakes, mayonnaise, corn syrup, honey, and mustard in a medium bowl. Refrigerate half of the sauce, covered. Save for later. Place a large skillet over medium heat and add oil. Add the chicken breasts in the hot oil and sauté until both sides are browned, or around 3 to 5 minutes per side. Transfer the chicken breasts to a 9 x 13-inch baking dish. Top each breast with honey mustard sauce, then with a layer of bacon and mushrooms. Sprinkle shredded cheese on top. Bake until the chicken's juices are clear and the cheese has melted, or around 15 minutes.

Garnish with parsley. Serve along with the honey mustard sauce.

Nutrition:

Calories: 813;   Total Carbohydrate: 57.1 g,

Cholesterol: 153 mg,   Total Fat: 46.1 g,

Protein: 47.2 g,   Sodium: 1807 mg

14. KFC Vegan Popcorn Chicken

Preparation time: 20 Minutes

Cooking time: 20 Minutes

Servings: 3-4 (2 cups)

Ingredients:

- Dried chunks of soy (2 cups)
- Grated ginger (1-inch cube)
- Minced garlic (2 cloves)
- Flour (.5 cup)
- Salt (1 tsp. /as required)
- Cornstarch (.5 cup)
- Vegetable broth - divided (3 cups + .75 cup)
- Breadcrumbs (1 cup)
- Garlic powder (1 tbsp.)
- Salt (.5 tsp.)
- Lemon pepper (1 tbsp.)

For the dip:

- Soy sour cream (.33 cup)
- Freshly chopped dill (1 tbsp.)
- Pepper (dash)

Directions:

Combine the chunks of soy, garlic, ginger, and salt in a bowl. Cover the chunks of soy using vegetable broth. Soak until the pieces are soft (20 minutes). Warm a pot with oil (1-inch) using a med-high temperature setting. Whisk the flour and vegetable broth from the soaking soy chunks until the lumps are removed. Add to the two bowls. Gently squeeze the excess liquid from the soy chunks using paper towels. Coat them in the bowl of the flour mixture. Transfer the chunks to a zipper-type bag with the cornstarch. Shake until coated. Toss into the second bowl of flour mixture and coat. Lastly, transfer to another zipper bag that has the breadcrumbs, garlic powder, salt, and lemon pepper. Fry in batches until golden. Drain on a layer of paper towels. Blend the sour cream, salt, pepper, and dill in a food processor to prepare the dip.

Nutrition:

Calorie: 226 g,   Fat: 0 g,   Carbs: 37.75,
Sodium: 1861 mg,   Protein: 11.2 g

15. Mediterranean Bowl

⏳**Preparation time:** 10 minutes

🕐**Cooking time:** 50 minutes

🍽**Servings:** 5

Ingredients:

- 5 chicken thighs, skin on, bone in
- 1/2 teaspoon salt
- 1 tablespoon dried oregano
- 1 to 2 lemons, you should use the zest and squeeze
- 4 tablespoon lemon juices
- 4 garlic cloves, minced
- 2 teaspoon black pepper
- 1 1/2 tablespoon olive oil, separated

- 1 small onion, finely diced
- 1 cup long grain rice
- 1 1/2 cups chicken broth
- 3/4 cup water
- 1 tablespoon dried oregano
- 3/4 teaspoon salt

Directions:

Start by placing the chicken in a Zip lock back along with lemon juice, lemon zest, oregano, cloves, and salt. Seal the bag and keep it aside. You can either set it aside for about 20 minutes or keep it refrigerated overnight. When you are ready to cook the chicken, then preheat the oven to 350° F. Remove the chicken from the zip lock bag but don't throw away the chicken marinade in the bag. Place a skillet over medium heat and pour ½ tablespoon of olive oil. Allow the oil to heat a little and then place the chicken with the skin side down. Cook the chicken until it turns golden brown and then flip it over. Cook until the other side turns golden brown as well. Take the chicken off the skillet and keep it aside. Remove the oil and fat from the skillet. Clean the skillet using a paper towel to remove any bits that might remain. Place it back over medium heat again.

Add the remaining olive oil into the skillet and increase the heat to medium high. Add onion and sauté until it becomes translucent. Add all the Ingredients for rice and the marinade as well into the skillet.

Reduce the heat to low and allow the Ingredients to simmer for about 30 seconds. Add the chicken on top and cover the skillet. Transfer the skillet into the oven and bake for about 35 minutes. Remove the lid and continue baking for about 10 minutes more or until the rice is tender and the liquid has been absorbed.

Remove from the oven and allow the dish to cool for about 5 to 10 minutes. Serve hot.

Nutrition:

Calories: 667,   Protein: 75 g,

Total Fat: 23 g,   Carbohydrate: 34 g

16. Cinnamon and Cayenne Chicken

Preparation time: 5 hours (including refrigeration time)

Cooking time: 1 hour

Servings: 6

Ingredients:

- 1 whole chicken (3.5 pounds)
- ¼ cup olive oil
- 1 tablespoon kosher salt
- 1 tablespoon ground coriander
- ¼ teaspoon ground cinnamon
- ⅛ teaspoon cayenne
- 2 tablespoons roughly chopped green olives
- 1 tablespoon chopped mint, plus more for garnish
- 8 dried figs, roughly chopped
- 2 tablespoons fresh lemon juice
- 1 cup chicken broth

- 2 tablespoons roughly chopped pitted Kalamata olives

Directions:

We are going to start by removing the backbone of the chicken. To do so, place it breast down on the chopping board. Remove the backbone using kitchen shears. Use your hands to flatten it into a butterfly shape. Take a small bowl and add coriander, salt, cinnamon, cayenne, and 2 tablespoons olive oil. Apply the mixture to both sides of the chicken. Place the chicken in an airtight container and refrigerate it for about 5 hours. You can even keep it refrigerated for about 24 hours if you are planning to have it for dinner the next day. Preheat the oven to 400° F.

Take a pan and place it over medium high heat. Pour olive oil and allow it to become hot.

Gently lower the chicken into the pan with the skin side down and cook until it turns golden brown. Place the pan into the oven and then bake for about 30 minutes. Take the pan out, turn over the chicken, and add mint, figs, olives, lemon juice, and chicken broth into the pan. Place the pan back into the oven and cook for another 30 minutes, or until the internal temperature reads 165° F. You can use a thermometer to check the temperature of the chicken. Take the chicken out, transfer to a plate, top with mint, and Serve with the fig mixture.

Nutrition:

Calories: 501,   Protein: 34 g,

Total Fat: 37 g,   Carbohydrate: 5 g

17. Red Lobster's Clam Chowder

Preparation time: 20 minutes

Cooking time: 30 minutes

Servings: 8

Ingredients:

- 2 tablespoons butter
- 1 cup onion, diced
- ½ cup leek, white part, thinly sliced
- ¼ teaspoon garlic, minced
- ½ cup celery, diced
- 2 tablespoons flour
- 4 cups milk
- 1 cup clams with juice, diced
- 1 cup potato, diced
- 1 tablespoon salt
- ¼ teaspoon white pepper
- 1 teaspoon dried thyme
- ½ cup heavy cream
- Saltine crackers for serving

Directions:

In a pot, sauté the onion, leek, garlic, and celery in butter over medium heat. After 3 minutes, remove the vegetables from the heat and add the flour. Whisk in the milk and clam juice. Return the mixture to the heat and bring it to a boil. Add the potatoes, salt, pepper, and thyme, and then lower the heat to let the mixture simmer. Continue mixing for another 10 minutes while the soup is simmering. Add in the clams and let the mixture simmer for 5 to 8 minutes, or until the clams are cooked. Add the heavy cream and cook for a few more minutes. Transfer the soup to a bowl and Serve with saltine crackers.

Nutrition:

Calories436.1,   Carbs30.1g,

Total Fat 26.5g,   Protein 20.3 g,   Sodium 1987 mg

18. Grilled Chicken Tenderloins

Preparation Time: 10 minutes

Cooking Time: 1 hour 10 minutes

Servings: 4

Ingredients:

- 1 lb. chicken tenders or cut chicken breasts
- 1/2 cup Italian dressing
- 2 tablespoons honey
- 2 teaspoons lime juice

Directions:

Place chicken tenderloins into a large plastic bag with wet ingredients. Marinate in refrigerator for at least one hour. Add chicken and liquid to a large skillet. Cook over medium heat until liquid is reduced, and chicken is golden in color, but not dry. Be sure to turn chicken throughout the cooking process.

Nutrition:

Calories: 201,   Carbohydrates: 3g,   Protein: 24g, Fat: 9g,   Saturated Fat: 1g,   Cholesterol: 72mg, Sodium: 423mg,   Sugar: 3g,   Potassium: 444mg

19. Sunday Fried Chicken

Preparation Time: 10 minutes

Cooking Time: 20 minutes

Servings: 4

Ingredients:

- oil for frying
- 4 boneless, skinless chicken breasts
- 2 cups all-purpose flour
- 2 teaspoons salt
- 2 teaspoons ground black pepper
- 1 cup buttermilk
- 1/2 cup water

Directions:

Pour 3 to 4 inches of oil into a deep fryer or large pot and preheat the oil to 350 degrees. Prepare seasoned flour by combining the flour, salt, and pepper in a bowl. Stir to combine well. In another bowl mix together the buttermilk and water. If your chicken breasts are not fairly uniform in size place them between two pieces of wax paper and gently pound them out with a meat pounder until they are more uniform in size.

This will help with even cooking times. Pat chicken breasts dry with a paper towel. Season the chicken with salt and pepper and then dredge into the flour, dip in buttermilk, and then dredge again in the seasoned flour and deep-fry the chicken pieces in the hot oil.

Turn the chicken breasts during the cooking to make sure that both sides of the chicken are golden brown. This should take 7 to 8 minutes for each one to cook. When the chicken is done, drain in a wire rack.

Nutrition:

Calories: 503,   Carbohydrates: 51g,

Protein: 8g, Fat: 29g, Saturated Fat: 23g, Sugar: 3g

Cholesterol: 7mg,   Sodium: 1229mg,

Potassium: 161mg,   Fiber: 1g,

20. Broccoli Cheddar Chicken

Preparation Time: 10 minutes

Cooking Time: 45 minutes

Servings: 4

Ingredients:

- 4 boneless skinless chicken breasts
- 1 can of Campbell's Cheddar Cheese Soup
- 1 cup milk
- 1 1/2 cups Ritz Crackers (one sleeve)
- 4 tablespoons of melted butter (you can use more)
- 8 ounces frozen broccoli
- 4 ounces shredded cheddar cheese
- 1/2 teaspoon seasoned salt

Directions:

Preheat your oven to 350 degrees. Make can of Cheddar cheese soup mix according to package directions (one can of soup mix to one can of milk). Place chicken breasts in a 9 by 13-inch baking dish. Season with seasoned salt.

Pour 3/4 of the prepared soup over the chicken breasts. Add broccoli to chicken that has been covered with the cheddar soup.

Melt butter and combine with Ritz crackers, sprinkle buttered crackers over the broccoli. Add remaining soup mix and bake for approximately 45 minutes or until the chicken is done. (Check chicken by cutting the thickest part and look to see that the chicken is uniform in color). When chicken has been removed from oven sprinkle with shredded cheddar cheese.

Nutrition:

Calories: 1354,   Carbohydrates: 91g, Protein: 86g, Fat: 67g,   Saturated Fat: 30g,   Cholesterol: 281mg, Sodium: 5234mg, Potassium: 4924mg,   Fiber: 8g, Sugar: 20g

21. Chicken Casserole

Preparation Time: 10 minutes

Cooking Time: 1 hour 5 minutes

Servings: 4

Ingredients:

- Corn bread
- 1 cup yellow cornmeal
- 1/3 cup all-purpose flour
- 1 1/2 teaspoon baking powder
- 1 tablespoon sugar
- 1/2 teaspoon salt
- 1/2 teaspoon baking soda
- 2 tablespoons vegetable oil
- 3/4 cup buttermilk
- 1 egg

- 1/2 cup melted butter

Chicken Filling:

- 2 tablespoons butter
- 1/4 cup chopped yellow onion
- 1/2 cup celery, thinly sliced
- 1 3/4 cup chicken broth
- 1 can cream of chicken soup
- 1 teaspoon salt
- 1/4 teaspoon pepper
- 2 1/2 cups cooked chicken breast, cut in bite-size pieces

Directions:

Corn bread mix all the ingredients for the cornbread except the melted butter together in a mixing bowl until smooth. Pour the batter into a greased 8-inch square baking pan and bake at 375 degrees F for 20 - 25 minutes or until golden and done. Remove from the oven and let cool completely. When the cornbread is cool, crumble all the cornbread and place 3 cups of the cornbread crumbs in a mixing bowl. Add the 1/2 cup melted butter to crumbs and mix well, set aside.

Chicken Filling:

In medium-sized saucepan on medium-low heat, heat the butter and sauté the chopped onions and celery until they are transparent, stirring occasionally. Add the chicken broth, cream of chicken soup, salt, and pepper. Stir until well blended and the soup is dissolved completely. Add the cooked chicken; stir and blend until mixture reaches a low simmer.

Cook for 5 minutes, then remove from the heat.

Place the chicken filling in a buttered 2 1/2-quart casserole dish or individual casserole dishes (about four). Sprinkle the cornbread crumb topping on top of the chicken mixture; do not stir into the chicken filling. It should form a crust over the filling. Place the baking dish in preheated oven at 350 degrees F for 35 - 40 minutes. The crumbs will turn a golden yellow. Serve while hot.

Nutrition:

Calories: 582,   Carbohydrates: 50g, Protein: 37g, Fat: 25g,   Saturated Fat: 13g,   Fiber: 4g, Cholesterol: 141mg,   Sodium: 2111mg, Sugar: 6g Potassium: 757mg

22. Chicken-Fried Steak & Gravy

Preparation Time: 15 minutes

Cooking Time: 10 minutes

Servings: 4

Ingredients:

- 1-1/4 cups all-purpose flour, divided
- 2 large eggs
- 1-1/2 cups 2% milk, divided
- 4 beef cube steaks (6 ounces each)
- 1-1/4 teaspoons salt, divided
- 1 teaspoon pepper, divided
- Oil for frying
- 1 cup water

Directions:

Place 1 cup flour in a shallow bowl. In a separate shallow bowl, whisk eggs and 1/2 cup milk until blended. Sprinkle steaks with 3/4 teaspoon each salt and pepper. Dip in flour to coat both sides; shake off excess. Dip in egg mixture, then again in flour. In a large cast-iron or other heavy skillet, heat 1/4 in. of oil over medium heat. Add steaks; cook until golden brown and a thermometer reads 160°, 4-6 minutes on each side. Remove from pan; drain on paper towels. Keep warm. Remove all but 2 tablespoons oil from pan. Stir in the remaining 1/4 cup flour, 1/2 teaspoon salt and 1/4 teaspoon pepper until smooth; cook and stir over medium heat until golden brown, 3-4 minutes. Gradually whisk in water and remaining milk. Bring to a boil, stirring constantly; cook and stir until thickened, 1-2 minutes. Serve with steaks.

Nutrition:

Calories: 563, Fat: 28g, Saturated fat: 5g, Cholesterol: 148mg, Sodium: 839mg, Sugars: 4g, Carbohydrate: 29g, Fiber: 1g, Protein: 46g

23. Spicy Oven-Fried Chicken

Preparation Time: 25 minutes

Cooking Time: 35 minutes

Servings: 8

Ingredients:

- 8 bone-in chicken breast halves, skin removed (8 ounces each)
- 2 cups buttermilk
- 2 tablespoons Dijon mustard
- 2 teaspoons salt
- 2 teaspoons hot pepper sauce
- 1-1/2 teaspoons garlic powder
- 2 cups soft breadcrumbs
- 1 cup cornmeal
- 2 tablespoons canola oil
- 1/2 teaspoon poultry seasoning
- 1/2 teaspoon ground mustard
- 1/2 teaspoon paprika
- 1/2 teaspoon cayenne pepper
- 1/4 teaspoon dried oregano
- 1/4 teaspoon dried parsley flakes

Directions:

Preheat oven to 400°. In a large bowl or dish, combine the first five ingredients. Add chicken and turn to coat. Refrigerate 1 hour or overnight. Drain chicken, discarding marinade. In a large bowl, combine remaining ingredients. Add chicken, one piece at a time, and coat with crumb mixture. Place on a parchment-lined baking sheet. Bake 35-40 minutes or until a thermometer reads 170°.

Nutrition:

Calories: 296,   Fat: 7g,   Sodium: 523mg
Cholesterol: 103mg,   Carbohydrate: 15g,
Protein: 40g

24. Skillet-Grilled Catfish

Preparation Time: 15 minutes

Cooking Time: 10 minutes

Servings: 4

Ingredients:

- 1/4 cup all-purpose flour
- 1/4 cup cornmeal
- 1 teaspoon onion powder
- 1 teaspoon dried basil
- 1/2 teaspoon garlic salt
- 1/2 teaspoon dried thyme
- 1/4 to 1/2 teaspoon white pepper
- 1/4 to 1/2 teaspoon cayenne pepper
- 1/4 to 1/2 teaspoon pepper
- 4 catfish fillets (6 to 8 ounces each)
- 1/4 cup butter

Directions:

In a large shallow dish, combine the first 9 ingredients. Add catfish, one fillet at a time, and turn to coat. Place a large cast-iron skillet on a grill rack over medium-high heat. Melt butter in the skillet; add catfish in batches, if necessary.

Grill, covered, until fish just begins to flake easily with a fork, 5-10 minutes on each side.

Nutrition:

Calories: 222,   Fat: 15g,   Sodium: 366mg
Cholesterol: 51mg, Carbohydrate: 14g,   Protein: 8g

25. Country Chicken with Gravy

Preparation Time: 5 minutes

Cooking Time: 25 minutes

Servings: 4

Ingredients:

- 3/4 cup crushed cornflakes
- 1/2 teaspoon poultry seasoning
- 1/2 teaspoon paprika
- 1/4 teaspoon salt
- 1/4 teaspoon dried thyme
- 1/4 teaspoon pepper
- 2 tablespoons fat-free evaporated milk
- 4 boneless skinless chicken breast halves (4 ounces each)
- 2 teaspoons canola oil

Gravy:

- 1 tablespoon butter
- 1 tablespoon all-purpose flour
- 1/4 teaspoon pepper
- 1/8 teaspoon salt
- 1/2 cup fat-free evaporated milk

- 1/4 cup condensed chicken broth, undiluted
- 1 teaspoon sherry or additional condensed chicken broth
- 2 tablespoons minced chives

Directions:

In a shallow bowl, combine the first six ingredients. Place milk in another shallow bowl. Dip chicken in milk, then roll in cornflake mixture. In a large nonstick skillet, cook chicken in oil over medium heat until a thermometer reads 170°, 6-8 minutes on each side. Meanwhile, in a small saucepan, melt butter. Stir in the flour, pepper, and salt until smooth. Gradually stir in the milk, broth, and sherry. Bring to a boil; cook and stir until thickened, 1-2 minutes. Stir in chives. Serve with chicken.

Nutrition:

Calories:274,   Fat:8g,   Cholesterol: 72mg,
Sodium: 569mg,   Carbohydrate: 20g,   Protein: 28g

26. Apple Cider BBQ Chicken Breast

Preparation Time: 20 minutes

Cooking Time: 3 ½ hours

Servings: 4

Ingredients:

- 1 tablespoon canola oil
- 4 bone-in chicken thighs (about 1-1/2 pounds), skin removed
- 1/4 teaspoon salt
- 1/4 teaspoon pepper 2 medium Fuji or Gala apples, coarsely chopped
- 1 medium onion, chopped
- 1 garlic clove, minced
- 1/3 cup barbecue sauce
- 1/4 cup apple cider or juice
- 1 tablespoon honey

Directions:

In a large skillet, heat oil over medium heat. Brown chicken thighs on both sides; sprinkle with salt and pepper. Transfer to a 3-qt. slow cooker; top with apples. Add onion to same skillet; cook and stir over medium heat 2-3 minutes or until tender. Add garlic; cook 1 minute longer. Stir in barbecue sauce, apple cider and honey; increase heat to medium-high. Cook 1 minute, stirring to loosen browned bits from pan. Pour over chicken and apples. Cook, covered, on low 3-1/2 to 4-1/2 hours or until chicken is tender. Freeze option: Freeze cooled chicken mixture in freezer containers. To use, partially thaw in refrigerator overnight. Heat through in a covered saucepan, stirring occasionally.

Nutrition:

Calories: 333,   Fat: 13g,   Protein: 25g
Cholesterol: 87mg,   Sodium: 456mg,
Carbohydrate: 29g,

27. Green Chili Jack Chicken

Preparation Time: 5 minutes

Cooking Time: 20 minutes

Servings: 2 to 3

Ingredients:

- 1 lb. chicken strips
- 1 teaspoon chili powder
- 4 ounces green chilies
- 1 cup Monterey jack cheese
- ¼ cup salsa

Directions:

Spray a medium size frypan with cooking spray. Sprinkle chili powder over chicken. Cook chicken strips until no longer pink. Turn stove top on low and add green chilis on top of chicken. Cook until chilis are warmed. Add cheese and cook until melted on top of chilis. Put on a dish and serve with salsa on the side.

Nutrition: Calories: 516, Total Fat: 24.4g, Sodium: 697.9mg, Saturated Fat: 12.6g, Cholesterol: 209mg, Protein:64.2g, Dietary Fiber: 1.8g, Sugars 4.3g, Total Carbohydrate:8.5g,

28. Orange Chicken

Preparation Time: 10 minutes

Cooking Time: 40 minutes

Servings: 4

Ingredients:

- ¾ cup fresh squeezed orange juice
- 1 ½ teaspoon orange zest, grated
- ¾ cup chicken broth, reduced sodium
- 8 strips of orange peel (each approximately 2" long and ½" wide)
- 1 ½ pounds chicken thighs; skinless trimmed & cut in 1 ½" pieces
- 6 tablespoon distilled white vinegar
- ¼ cup soy sauce
- 8 small whole dried red chilies, optional
- ½ cup dark brown sugar, packed
- 1 tablespoon plus
- 2 teaspoon cornstarch
- 3 garlic cloves, pressed or minced
- 1-piece (1") ginger, grated
- 2 tablespoon cold water

- ¼ teaspoon cayenne pepper

For Coating & Frying:

- 1 cup cornstarch
- 3 large egg whites
- ¼ teaspoon cayenne pepper
- 3 cups peanut oil
- ½ teaspoon baking soda

Directions:

For the Marinade & Sauce:

Place the chicken thighs in a one-gallon zipper-lock bag; set aside. Now, combine the chicken broth together with grated zest, orange juice, ginger, soy sauce, vinegar, garlic, cayenne & sugar in large-sized saucepan; whisk until the sugar is completely dissolved. Measure approximately ¾ cup of the prepared mixture out & pour into the bag with chicken; press out the air as much as possible & seal the bag; ensure that the pieces are coated well with the marinade. Refrigerate for 30 to 60 minutes. Bring the leftover mixture to a boil over high heat in the saucepan. Stir the cornstarch with cold water in a small bowl; whisk the cornstarch mixture into the sauce. Let the sauce to simmer for a minute, until thick & translucent, stirring occasionally. Turn off the heat and then stir in the orange peel & chilies; set the sauce aside.

For the Coating:

Place the egg whites in a pie plate; beat using a large fork until completely frothy. Whisk the cornstarch together with cayenne & baking soda in a second pie plate until combined well. Drain the chicken in a large mesh strainer or colander; thoroughly pat the chicken dry using paper towels. Place half of chicken pieces into the egg whites; turn to coat and then transfer the pieces to the cornstarch mixture; ensure that the pieces are thoroughly coated. Place the dredged chicken pieces on a wire rack set over the baking sheet; repeat with the leftover chicken pieces.

For the Chicken:

Now, over high heat in straight-sided sauté pan or 11 to 12" Dutch oven; heat up the oil until hot. Work in batches & carefully place half of the chicken into the oil one piece at a time; fry for a couple of minutes, until turn golden brown, turning each piece with tongs halfway during the cooking process. Transfer the chicken to a paper towels lined large plate.

Heat up the oil & repeat the steps with the leftover chicken.

To Serve:

Reheat the sauce over medium heat for approximately 2 minutes, until simmering. Add in the chicken & toss gently until coated evenly & heated through. Serve immediately and enjoy.

Nutrition:

Calories:490,   Total   Fat:23g,   Sugars:19g, Cholesterol: 80 mg,   Sodium:820 mg, Protein: 25g Total Carbohydrate: 51 g,   Dietary Fiber: 2 g,

29. Fish Tacos

Preparation Time: 10 minutes

Cooking Time: 30 minutes

Servings: 4

Ingredients:

- 1-pound halibut fillet, skin removed
- ¼ green cabbage
- 10 corn tortillas, warmed
- ¼ cup white onion, chopped

Salsa:

- Juice of 1 lime, freshly squeezed
- ¼ cup English cucumber, chopped

Guacamole:

- ½ bunch of fresh cilantros, chopped
- 1 tablespoon olive oil
- Pepper & salt to taste

Directions:

For Cabbage Slaw:

In a large bowl add the chiffonade cabbage together with cucumber, onion & cilantro; squeeze the lime juice on top & toss well;sprinkle pepper & salt to taste; let sit for 30 minutes at room temperature.

Preheat your oven to 400 F. Over medium heat in a non-stick oven proof pan; heat up the olive oil until hot and then carefully add the halibut; cook until the first side turn brown; turn over & put the pan in the preheated oven until the halibut is flakey & cooked through, for 10 to 15 minutes. Flake the cooked halibut into a bowl & serve with warmed corn tortillas & the bowls of the guacamole, cabbage slaw & salsa. Enjoy.

Nutrition:

Calories: 230,   Total Fat: 12g,   Sugar: 2g,
Cholesterol: 15 mg,   Sodium: 470 mg,   Protein:7g,
Total Carbohydrate: 26 g,   Dietary Fiber: 3 g

30. Chicken Fried Chicken

Preparation time: 15 minutes

Cooking time: 30 minutes

Servings: 4

Ingredients:

Chicken:

- ½ cup all-purpose flour
- 1 teaspoon poultry seasoning
- ½ teaspoon salt
- ½ teaspoon pepper
- 1 egg, slightly beaten
- 1 tablespoon water
- 4 boneless skinless chicken breasts, pounded to ½-inch thickness
- 1 cup vegetable oil

Gravy:

- 2 tablespoons all-purpose flour
- ¼ teaspoon salt
- ¼ teaspoon pepper
- 1¼ cups milk

Directions:

Preheat the oven to 200°F. In a shallow dish, combine the flour, poultry seasoning, salt and pepper. In another shallow dish, mix together the beaten egg and water. First dip both sides of the chicken breasts in the flour mixture, then dip them in the egg mixture, and then back into the flour mixture. Heat the vegetable oil over medium-high heat in a large deep skillet. A cast iron is good choice if you have one. Add the chicken and cook for about 15 minutes or until fully cooked, turning over about halfway through. Transfer the chicken to a cookie sheet and place in the oven to maintain temperature. Remove all but 2 tablespoons of oil from the skillet you cooked the chicken in. Prepare the gravy by whisking the dry gravy Ingredients together in a bowl. Then whisk them into the oil in the skillet, stirring thoroughly to remove lumps. When the flour begins to brown, slowly whisk in the milk. Continue cooking and whisking for about 2 minutes or until the mixture thickens. Top the chicken with some of the gravy.

Nutrition:

Calories: 234, Fat: 24 g, Carbs: 54 g, Protein: 61 g, Sodium: 1286 mg

31. Sunday Chicken

Preparation time: 10 minutes

Cooking time: 10 minutes

Servings: 4

Ingredients:

- Oil for frying
- 4 boneless, skinless chicken breasts
- 1 cups all-purpose flour
- 1 cup bread crumbs
- 2 teaspoons salt
- 2 teaspoons black pepper
- 1 cup buttermilk
- ½ cup water

Directions:

Add 3–4 inches of oil to a large pot or a deep fryer and preheat to 350°F. Mix together the flour, breadcrumbs, salt and pepper in a shallow dish. To a separate shallow dish, add the buttermilk and water; stir. Pound the chicken breasts to a consistent size. Dry them with a paper towel, then sprinkle with salt and pepper. Dip the seasoned breasts in the flour mixture, then the buttermilk mixture, and then back into the flour. Add the breaded chicken to the hot oil and fry for about 8 minutes. Turn the chicken as necessary so that it cooks evenly on both sides. Remove the chicken to either a wire rack or a plate lined with paper towels to drain. Serve with mashed potatoes or whatever sides you love.

Nutrition:

Calories: 265, Fat: 47.9 g, Carbs: 65. 5 g, Protein: 37. 4 g, Sodium: 454 mg

32. Campfire Chicken

Preparation time: 10 minutes

Cooking time: 45 minutes

Servings: 4

Ingredients:

- 1 tablespoon paprika
- 2 teaspoons onion powder
- 2 teaspoons salt
- 1 teaspoon garlic powder
- 1 teaspoon dried rosemary
- 1 teaspoon black pepper
- 1 teaspoon dried oregano
- 1 whole chicken, quartered
- 2 carrots cut into thirds
- 3 red skin potatoes, halved
- 1 ear of corn, quartered
- 1 tablespoon olive oil
- 1 tablespoon butter
- 5 sprigs fresh thyme

Directions:

Preheat the oven to 400°F. In a small bowl, combine the paprika, onion powder, salt, garlic powder, rosemary, pepper and oregano. Add the chicken quarters and 1 tablespoon of the spice mix to a large plastic freezer bag. Seal and refrigerate for at least 1 hour. Add the corn, carrots and potatoes to a large bowl. Drizzle with the olive oil and remaining spice mix. Stir or toss to coat. Preheat a large skillet over high heat. Add some oil, and when it is hot, add the chicken pieces and cook until golden brown. Lay out 4 pieces of aluminum foil and add some carrots, potatoes, corn and a chicken quarter to each. Top with some butter and thyme. Fold the foil in and make pouches by sealing the edges tightly.

Bake for 45 minutes.

Nutrition:

Calories: 234, Fat: 54. 4 g, Carbs: 67. 9 g, Protein: 76. 5, Sodium: 652 mg

33. Alice Springs Chicken from Outback

Preparation time: 5 minutes

Cooking time: 2 hours and 30 minutes

Servings: 4

Ingredients:

Sauce:

- ½ cup Dijon mustard
- ½ cup honey
- ¼ cup mayonnaise
- 1 teaspoon fresh lemon juice
- 4 chicken breast, boneless and skinless
- 2 tablespoons butter
- 1 tablespoon olive oil
- 8 ounces fresh mushrooms, sliced
- 4 slices bacon, cooked and cut into 2-inch pieces
- 2 ½ cups Monterrey Jack cheese, shredded
- Parsley for serving (optional)

Directions:

Preheat oven to 400 °F. Mix together ingredients for the sauce in a bowl. Put chicken in a Ziploc bag, and then add sauce into bag until only ¼ cup is left.

 Keep remaining sauce in a container, cover, and refrigerate. Make sure to seal Ziploc bag tightly and shake gently until chicken is coated with sauce Keep in refrigerator for at least 2 hours. Melt butter in a pan over medium heat. Toss in mushrooms and cook for 5 minutes or until brown. Remove from pan and place on a plate. In an oven-safe pan, heat oil. Place marinated chicken flat in pan and cook for 5 minutes on each side or until both sides turn golden brown.

Nutrition:

Calories: 888,   Fat: 56 g,   Carbs: 41 g,
Protein: 59 g,   Sodium: 1043 mg

34. Panda Express' Orange Chicken

Preparation time: 15 minutes

Cooking time: 30 minutes

Servings: 6

Ingredients:

Orange sauce:

- ¼ cup flour
- 1½ tablespoon soy sauce
- 1½ tablespoon water
- 5 tablespoons sugar
- 5 tablespoons white vinegar
- 3 tablespoons orange zest
- 1 egg -
- 1½ teaspoon salt
- White pepper, to taste
- 5 tablespoons grape seed oil, divided
- ½ cup + 1 tablespoon cornstarch
- ¼ cup cold water

- 2 pounds chicken breast, boneless and skinless, chopped
- 1 teaspoon fresh ginger, grated
- 1 teaspoon garlic, finely chopped
- ½ teaspoon hot red chili pepper, ground
- ¼ cup green onion, sliced
- 1 tablespoon rice wine
- ½ teaspoon sesame oil
- White rice and steamed broccoli for serving

Directions:

Mix together ingredients for the orange sauce in a bowl. Reserve for later. Add egg, salt, pepper, and 1 tablespoon oil to a separate bowl. Mix well. In another bowl, combine ½ cup cornstarch and flour. Mix until fully blended. Add remaining cornstarch and cold water in a different bowl. Blend until cornstarch is completely dissolved. Heat 3 tablespoons oil in a large deep skillet or wok over high heat. Coat chicken pieces in egg mixture. Let excess drip off. Then, coat in cornstarch mixture. Cook for at least 3 minutes or until both sides are golden brown and chicken is cooked through. Arrange on a plate lined with paper towels to drain excess oil.

In a clean large deep skillet, or wok heat remaining oil on high heat. Lightly sauté ginger and garlic for 30 seconds or until aromatic.

Toss in peppers and green onions.

Stir-fry vegetables for 1-3 minutes, and then pour in rice wine. Mix well before adding orange sauce. Bring to a boil. Mix in cooked chicken pieces, and then add cornstarch mixture. Simmer until mixture is thick, and then mix in sesame oil. Transfer onto a plate and serve with white rice and steamed broccoli.

Nutrition:

Calories: 305, Fat: 5 g, Carbs: 27 g,
Protein: 34 g, Sodium: 1024 mg

35. Shrimp with Lobster Sauce

Preparation time: 10 minutes

Cooking time: 10 minutes

Servings: 4

Ingredients:

- ½-1½ lbs. raw large shrimp, peeled/shelled, tails off and deveined
- 1.5 cups lobster broth
- ½ Tbsp low sodium soy sauce
- ½ Tbsp Shaoxing wine
- 1 tsp. of sugar
- ½ tsp. white pepper
- ½ Tbsp crushed ginger
- ½ Tbsp crushed garlic
- 1.5 cups frozen peas
- 1 bunch of scallions, sliced
- 3 tablespoon cornstarch
- 3 tablespoons water

- 2 egg whites without yolks, beaten
- ½ Tbsp of heavy cream

Directions:

Add the lobster broth, Shaoxing wine, soy sauce, ginger, garlic, sugar and white pepper to the pot. Mix well Add the shrimp. Mix well. Lock the lid. Turn the valve to Sealing. Set to 0 minutes of high pressure. Do a quick-release. Meanwhile, beat the egg whites. Make a cornstarch slurry to thicken the sauce. Transfer the shrimp to a serving plate. Set to Sauté (High) and let it boil. Add the frozen peas and scallions and mix well. When it starts bubbling, add the cornstarch slurry and mix for 1 minute. Turn off and let it cool down. When it has stopped bubbling, add beaten egg whites and stir. Add the heavy cream and give it a stir.

Serve the shrimp with the sauce.

Nutrition:

Carbohydrates:10 g,   Protein: 31 g,

Fat: 11 g,   Calories: 270g

36. Panko-Crusted Cod

Preparation time: 10 minutes

Cooking time: 10 minutes

Servings: 4

Ingredients:

- ½ cup panko bread crumbs
- 2 Tbsp extra-virgin olive oil
- 2 tsp. grated lemon zest
- ¼ tsp. salt ¼ cup light mayonnaise
- 2 tsp. lemon juice
- ½ tsp. dried thyme
- 4 6 oz. cod fillets
- 1 cup Water
- 1 lemon cut into
- 4 wedges

Directions:

Set to Sauté (High) and heat the pot.

Add the bread crumbs and sauté for 2 minutes, stirring frequently. Add the oil, lemon zest, and salt. Transfer to a plate and set aside. Mix the mayonnaise, lemon juice, and thyme in a bowl.

Spread the mixture over the top of the cod fillets.

Pour water into the pot and put the fish into the steamer basket, mayonnaise side up. Lock the lid and set to 3 minutes of Manual. Do a quick-release. Serve the fish topped with the bread crumb mixture and lemon wedges.

Nutrition:

Carbohydrates: 10 g,

Fat: 11 g,

Protein: 31 g,

Calories: 270

37. Classic BBQ Chicken

Preparation time: 5 minutes

Cooking time: 1 hour 45 minutes

Servings: 4-6

Ingredients:

- 4 pounds of your favorite chicken, including legs, thighs, wings, and breasts, skin-on
- Salt
- Olive oil
- 1 cup barbecue sauce, like Hickory Mesquite or homemade

Directions:

Rub the chicken with olive oil and salt. Preheat the griddle to high heat. Sear chicken skin side down on the grill for 5-10 minutes. Turn the griddle down to medium low heat, tent with foil and cook for 30 minutes. Turn chicken and baste with barbecue sauce. Cover the chicken again and allow to cook for another 20 minutes. Baste, cover and cook again for 30 minutes; repeat basting and turning during this time. The chicken is done when the internal temperature of the chicken pieces is 165°F and juices run clear. Baste with more barbecue sauce to Serve!

Nutrition:

Calories: 539,   Sodium: 684mg,   Protein: 87.6 g

Dietary Fiber: 0.3g,   Fat: 11.6g,   Carbs: 15.1 g,

38. Grilled Sweet Chili Lime Chicken

Preparation time: 35 minutes

Cooking time: 15 minutes

Servings: 4

Ingredients:

- ½ cup sweet chili sauce
- ¼ cup soy sauce
- 1 teaspoon mirin
- 1 teaspoon orange juice, fresh squeezed
- 1 teaspoon orange marmalade
- 2 tablespoons lime juice
- 1 tablespoon brown sugar
- 1 clove garlic, minced
- 4 boneless, skinless chicken breasts
- Sesame seeds, for garnish

Directions:

Whisk sweet chili sauce, soy sauce, mirin, orange marmalade, lime and orange juice, brown sugar, and minced garlic together in a small mixing bowl.

Set aside ¼ cup of the sauce. Toss chicken in sauce to coat and marinate 30 minutes.

Preheat your griddle to medium heat. Put the chicken on the grill and grill each side for 7 minutes. Baste the cooked chicken with remaining marinade and garnish with sesame seeds to Serve with your favorite sides.

Nutrition:

Calories: 380,   Sodium: 1274mg,   Fat: 12g, Dietary Fiber: 0.5g,   Carbs: 19.7g,   Protein: 43.8 g

39. Chipotle Adobe Chicken

Preparation time: 1 - 24 hours

Cooking time: 20 minutes

Servings: 4 – 6

Ingredients:

- 2 lbs. chicken thighs or breasts (boneless, skinless)

For the marinade:

- ¼ cup olive oil
- 2 chipotle peppers, in adobo sauce, plus
- 1 teaspoon adobo sauce from the can
- 1 tablespoon garlic, minced
- 1 shallot, finely chopped
- 1 ½ tablespoons cumin
- 1 tablespoon cilantro, super-finely chopped or dried
- 2 teaspoons chili powder
- 1 teaspoon dried oregano
- 1/2 teaspoon salt
- Fresh limes, garnish
- Cilantro, garnish

Directions:

Preheat grill to medium-high. Add marinade Ingredients to a food processor or blender and pulse into a paste. Add the chicken and marinade to a sealable plastic bag and massage to coat well. Place in the refrigerator for 1 hour to 24 hours before grilling. Grill the chicken for 7 minutes, turn and grill and additional 7 minutes; or until good grill marks appear. Turn heat to low and continue to grill until chicken is cooked through and internal temperature reaches 165°F. Remove the chicken from the grill and allow to rest 5 to 10 minutes before serving. Garnish with a squeeze of fresh lime and a sprinkle of cilantro to Serve.

Nutrition:

Calories: 561,   Sodium: 431 mg,   Fat: 23.8 g,
Dietary Fiber: 0.3 g, Carbs: 18.7 g,   Protein: 65.9 g

40. Grilled Sweet Chili Lime Chicken

Preparation time: 8 - 24 hours

Cooking time: 20 minutes

Servings: 4

Ingredients:

- 2 lbs. boneless, skinless chicken thighs

For the marinade:

- 1/4 cup fresh lime juice
- 2 teaspoon lime zest
- 1/4 cup honey
- 2 tablespoons olive oil
- 1 tablespoon balsamic vinegar
- 1/2 teaspoon sea salt
- 1/2 teaspoon black pepper
- 2 garlic cloves, minced
- 1/4 teaspoon onion powder

Directions:

Whisk together marinade Ingredients in a large mixing bowl; reserve 2 tablespoons of the marinade for grilling. Add chicken and marinade to a sealable plastic bag and marinate 8 hours or overnight in the refrigerator. Preheat grill to medium high heat and brush lightly with olive oil. Place the chicken on the grill and cook 8 minutes per side. Baste each side of chicken with reserved marinade during the last few minutes of cooking; the chicken is done when the internal temperature reaches 165°F. Plate the chicken, tent with foil, and allow resting for 5 minutes. Serve and enjoy!

Nutrition:

Calories:381, Sodium: 337mg, Carbs: 4.7g
Fat: 20.2g, Dietary Fiber: 1.1g, Protein: 44.7 g.

41. Honey Balsamic Marinated Chicken

⏳ **Preparation time:** 30 minutes - 4 hours

🕐 **Cooking time:** 20 minutes

🍴 **Servings:** 4

Ingredients:

- 2 lbs. boneless, skinless chicken thighs
- 1 teaspoon olive oil
- 1/2 teaspoon sea salt
- 1/4 teaspoon black pepper
- 1/2 teaspoon paprika
- 3/4 teaspoon onion powder

For the Marinade:

- 2 tablespoons honey
- 2 tablespoons balsamic vinegar
- 2 tablespoons tomato paste
- 1 teaspoon garlic, minced

Directions:

Add chicken, olive oil, salt, black pepper, paprika, and onion powder to a sealable plastic bag. Seal and toss

---

to coat, covering the chicken with spices and oil; set aside. Whisk together balsamic vinegar, tomato paste, garlic, and honey. Divide the marinade in half. Add one half to the bag of chicken and store the other half in a sealed container in the refrigerator. Seal the bag and toss the chicken to coat. Refrigerate for 30 minutes to 4 hours. Preheat a grill to medium-high. Discard bag and marinade. Add the chicken to the grill and cook 7 minutes per side or until juices run clear and a meat thermometer reads 165°F. During last minute of cooking, brush remaining marinade on top of the chicken thighs. Serve immediately!

Nutrition:

Calories: 485,   Carbs: 11 g,   Sodium: 438 mg, Dietary Fiber: 0.5 g,   Fat: 18.1 g,   Protein: 66.1 g.

42. California Grilled Chicken

Preparation time: 35 minutes

Cooking time: 20 minutes

Servings: 4

Ingredients:

- 4 boneless, skinless chicken breasts
- 3/4 cup balsamic vinegar
- 2 tablespoons extra virgin olive oil
- 1 tablespoon honey
- 1 teaspoon oregano
- 1 teaspoon basil
- 1 teaspoon garlic powder

For garnish:

- Sea salt
- Black pepper, fresh ground
- 4 slices fresh mozzarella cheese
- 4 slices avocado
- 4 slices beefsteak tomato
- Balsamic glaze, for drizzling

Directions:

Whisk together balsamic vinegar, honey, olive oil, oregano, basil and garlic powder in a large mixing bowl. Add chicken to coat and marinate for 30 minutes in the refrigerator. Preheat grill to medium-high. Grill chicken for 7 minutes per side, or until a meat thermometer reaches 165°F. Top each chicken breast with mozzarella, avocado, and tomato and tent with foil on the grill to melt for 2 minutes. Garnish with a drizzle of balsamic glaze, and a pinch of sea salt and black pepper.

Nutrition:

Calories: 883,   Sodium: 449 mg,   Fat: 62.1g,
Dietary Fiber: 15.2g,   Protein: 55.3 g,   Carbs: 29.8g

43. Salsa Verde Marinated Chicken

⏳ **Preparation time:** 4 hours 35 minutes

🕐 **Cooking time:** 4 hours 50 minutes

🍽 **Servings:** 6

Ingredients:

- 6 boneless, skinless chicken breasts
- 1 tablespoon olive oil
- 1 teaspoon sea salt
- 1 teaspoon chili powder
- 1 teaspoon ground cumin
- 1 teaspoon garlic powder

For the salsa Verde marinade:

- 3 teaspoons garlic, minced
- 1 small onion, chopped
- 6 tomatillos, husked, rinsed and chopped
- 1 medium jalapeño pepper, cut in half, seeded
- ¼ cup fresh cilantro, chopped
- ½ teaspoon sugar or sugar substitute

Directions:

Add salsa Verde marinade Ingredients to a food processor and pulse until smooth. Mix sea salt, chili powder, cumin, and garlic powder together in a small mixing bowl. Season chicken breasts with olive oil and seasoning mix, and lay in glass baking dish. Spread a tablespoon of salsa Verde marinade over each chicken breast to cover; reserve remaining salsa for serving. Cover dish with plastic wrap and refrigerate for 4 hours. Preheat grill to medium-high and brush with olive oil. Add the chicken to the grill and cook 7 minutes per side or until juices run clear and a meat thermometer reads 165°F. Serve each with additional salsa Verde and enjoy!

Nutrition:

Calories: 321, Sodium: 444 mg, Carbs: 4.8 g, Dietary Fiber: 1.3g, Protein: 43g, Fat: 13.7g

44. Hawaiian Chicken Skewers

Preparation time: 1 hour 10 minutes

Cooking time: 15 minutes

Servings: 4 - 5

Ingredients:

- 1 lb. boneless, skinless chicken breast, cut into 1 ½ inch cubes
- 3 cups pineapple, cut into 1 ½ inch cubes
- 2 large green peppers, cut into 1 ½ inch pieces
- 1 large red onion, cut into 1 ½ inch pieces
- 2 tablespoons olive oil, to coat veggies

For the marinade:

- 1/3 cup tomato paste
- 1/3 cup brown sugar, packed
- 1/3 cup soy sauce
- 1/4 cup pineapple juice
- 2 tablespoons olive oil
- 1 1/2 tablespoon mirin or rice wine vinegar
- 4 teaspoons garlic cloves, minced
- 1 tablespoon ginger, minced
- 1/2 teaspoon sesame oil

- Pinch of sea salt
- Pinch of ground black pepper
- 10 wooden skewers, for assembly

Directions:

Combine marinade Ingredients in a mixing bowl until smooth. Reserve a 1/2 cup of the marinade in the refrigerator. Add the chicken and remaining marinade to a sealable plastic bag and refrigerate for 1 hour. Soak 10 wooden skewer sticks in water for 1 hour. Preheat the grill to medium heat. Add red onion, bell pepper and pineapple to a mixing bowl with 2 tablespoons olive oil and toss to coat. Thread red onion, bell pepper, pineapple and chicken onto the skewers until all of the chicken has been used. Place skewers on grill and grab your reserve marinade from the refrigerator; grill for 5 minutes then brush with remaining marinade and rotate. Brush again with marinade and grill about 5 additional minutes or until chicken reads 165°F on a meat thermometer. Serve warm.

Nutrition:

Calories: 311,   Fat: 8.8 g,   Sodium: 1116 mg,
Dietary Fiber: 4.2g,   Carbs: 38.1g,   Protein: 22.8g

45. Classic Cheesy Italian Arancini

Preparation time: 15 minutes

Cooking time: 30 minutes

Servings: 2

Ingredients:

- ½ cup white rice
- 1½ cups chicken broth
- Sea salt and ground black pepper, to taste
- 2 tablespoons Parmesan cheese, grated
- ½ tablespoon all-purpose flour
- 2 eggs
- 1 cup fresh bread crumbs
- ½ teaspoon oregano
- 1 teaspoon olive oil
- 1 teaspoon basil

Directions:

In a saucepan, cook the chicken broth until it boils over medium-high heat. Add the rice and lower the heat to simmer for around 20 minutes. Discard the broth. Transfer the rice to a bowl. Drain the excess water and let stand for a few minutes.

Add the salt, black pepper, Parmesan cheese, and flour. Stir to combine well. Scoop the mixture out and form into bite-sized balls on a clean work surface. Whisk the eggs in a separate bowl. Combine well the bread crumbs with the oregano, olive oil, and basil in a third bowl. Set aside. To make the Italian arancini, dip each rice ball into the eggs, then into the bread crumb mixture. Press to make them firm. Arrange the Italian arancini in the air fryer basket. Put the air fryer lid on and cook in the preheated instant pot at 350ºF for 10 to 12 minutes, turning the Italian arancini over once when it shows 'TURN FOOD' on the air fryer lid screen. Remove the Italian arancini from the basket and Serve warm.

Nutrition:

Calories: 349,   Fat: 7.4g,   Carbs: 52.1g,

Protein: 15.7g,   Sugars: 2.3g

46. Pot-Roast Chicken with Stock

Preparation Time: 10 mins

Cooking Time: 2 hrs and 10 mins

Serves: 4 with leftovers

Ingredients:

- 2 tbsp olive oil
- 2.4kg chicken – buy the best you can afford
- 4 onions, peeled and cut into large wedges
- ½ bunch thyme
- 3 garlic cloves
- 6 peppercorns
- 175ml white wine
- 1.2l chicken stock

Directions:

Heat oven to 170C/150C fan/gas 5. Heat the oil in a large flameproof casserole dish and brown the chicken well on all sides, then sit it breast-side up. Pack in the onions, thyme, garlic and peppercorns, pour over the wine and stock, and bring to the boil. Pop on the lid and transfer to the oven for 2 hrs. Remove and rest for 20 mins. Carefully lift the chicken onto a chopping board and carve as much as you need.

Serve the carved chicken in a shallow bowl with the onions and some of the stock poured over. Serve with some usual Sunday veg and roast potatoes. Strain the leftover stock into a bowl and strip the carcass of all the chicken. Chill both for up to three days or freeze for up to a month to use for other recipes like our one-pot chicken noodle soup.

Nutrition:

Kcal 500,   Fat: 29g,   Saturates: 7g,   Carbs: 6g, Sugars: 5g,   Fibre 2g,   Salt: 0.6g,   Protein: 51g,

47. Fish Pie Mac 'n' Cheese

Preparation Time: 10 mins

Cooking Time: 40 mins

Serves: 6 (or 4 adults and 4 children)

Ingredients:

- 650ml milk
- 40g plain flour
- 40g butter
- 2 tsp Dijon mustard
- 150g mature cheddar , grated
- 180g frozen peas
- handful of parsley , chopped
- 300g macaroni
- 300g fish pie mix (smoked fish, white fish and salmon)
- green salad , to serve (optional)

Directions:

Pour the milk into a large pan and add the flour and butter. Set over a medium heat and whisk continuously until you have a smooth, thick white sauce. Remove from the heat, add the mustard, most of the cheese (save a handful for the top), peas and parsley. Meanwhile, boil the pasta in a large pan of water following pack instructions until just cooked. Drain. Heat the oven to 200C/180C fan/gas 6. Tip the pasta into the sauce and add half the fish, stir everything together then tip into a large baking dish. Top with the rest of the fish, pushing it into the pasta a little, then scatter with the remaining cheese. Bake for 30 mins until golden, then serve with salad, if you like. Can be chilled and eaten within three days or frozen for up to a month. Defrost in the fridge, then reheat in a microwave or oven until piping hot.

Nutrition:

Kcal 504,   Fat: 22g,   Saturates: 12g,   Salt: 1.1g, Carbs: 47g,   Sugars: 8g,   Fibre: 5g,   Protein: 28g

48. Fish & Chip Traybake

Preparation Time: 20 mins

Cooking Time: 35 mins

Serves: 4

Ingredients:

- 2 large sweet potatoes , cut into thin wedges
- 1 tbsp rapeseed oil
- 4 tbsp fat-free natural yogurt
- 2 tbsp low-fat mayonnaise
- 3 cornichons , finely chopped, plus 1 tbsp of the brine
- 1 shallot , finely chopped
- 1 tbsp finely chopped dill , plus extra to serve
- 300g frozen peas
- 50ml milk
- 1 tbsp finely chopped mint
- 4 cod or pollock loin fillets
- 1 lemon , cut into wedges, to serve

Directions:

Heat the oven to 220C/200C fan/gas 8. Toss the sweet potatoes with the oil and some seasoning on a baking tray.

Roast for 20 mins. Combine the yogurt, mayonnaise, cornichons and reserved brine, the shallot and dill with 1 tbsp cold water in a small bowl and set aside. Meanwhile, put the peas in a pan with the milk, bring to a simmer and cook for 5 mins. Blitz the mixture using a hand blender until roughly puréed. Stir in the mint and season to taste. Set aside. Add the cod or pollock to the baking tray with the sweet potatoes, season and cook for 10-15 mins more, or until cooked through. Warm through the pea mixture. Scatter over some dill and serve the traybake with the yogurt tartare and the mushy peas.

Nutrition:

Kcal 396,   Fat: 9g,   Saturates: 1g,

Carbs: 37g,   Sugars: 21g,   Fibre: 8g,

Protein: 37g,   Salt 0.6g

49. Herby Fish Fingers with Chinese-Style Rice

Preparation Time: 10 mins

Cooking Time: 35 mins

Serves: 2

Ingredients:

- 100g brown basmati rice
- 160g frozen peas
- 50g French beans
- 3 spring onions , finely chopped
- ½ tsp dried chilli flakes
- good handful coriander , roughly chopped
- 2 tsp tamari
- few drops sesame oil
- 1 tbsp cold-pressed rapeseed oil
- 2 large eggs
- 280g pack skinless cod loins cut into chunky strips (cut into 4 strips per loin)

Directions:

Cook the rice in a pan of water for 25 mins, adding

the peas and beans for the last 6 mins. Drain, then return to the pan and stir in the spring onions, chilli flakes, all but 1 tbsp chopped coriander, the tamari and sesame oil. Cover. Meanwhile, heat a large non-stick pan with the rapeseed oil Beat the eggs with the remaining 1 tbsp coriander. Cut the fish into chunky strips, then coat them in the egg and fry in the oil for a couple of mins each side until golden.

Remove the fish from the pan and tip in the rice with any remaining egg and stir. Serve in bowls, topped with the fish.

Nutrition:

Kcal: 487,   Fat: 14g,   Saturates: 2g,   Carbs: 47g,
Sugars: 7g,   Fibre: 7g,   Protein: 40g,
Low in salt: 1.14g

50. White Fish with Sesame Noodles

⏳ **Preparation Time:** 10 mins

🕐 **Cooking Time:** 10 mins

🍽️ **Serves:** 2

Ingredients:

- 150g soba or whole meal noodles (300g if using pre-cooked)
- 25g toasted sesame seeds , plus extra to serve
- 2 tbsp soy sauce
- 1 tbsp oil
- 1 tsp rice vinegar (or any white vinegar)
- 200g spinach leaves

- 2 seabass fillets

Directions:

Use a spice grinder or pestle and mortar to crush the sesame seeds, then stir in the soy sauce, oil, 1 tbsp of water and a splash of rice vinegar, to make a creamy dressing, season and set aside.

Bring a pan of salted water to the boil, add the noodles and cook following pack instructions, then drain and set aside. Using the same pan, tip in all the spinach and cook until reduced down and dark green. Tip in the noodles, along with the sesame dressing and a splash of water and toss well to heat through. Heat the oil in a non-stick frying pan over a medium to high heat.

Season the skin of the seabass, then place in the pan skin-side down, fry until the skin has crisped up and the flesh has nearly all turned opaque, around 3 mins. Flip over and fry for 30 seconds further, until the fish is flaking and cooked through.

Divide the noodles and greens between two bowls and place the fish on top. Scatter over the toasted sesame seeds and serve.

Nutrition:

Kcal 624,   Fat: 24g,   Saturates: 4g,

Carbs: 54g,   Sugars: 3g,   Fibre: 7g,

Protein: 45g,   Salt: 4.1g

CPSIA information can be obtained
at www.ICGtesting.com
Printed in the USA
BVHW091938180521
607636BV00009B/1052